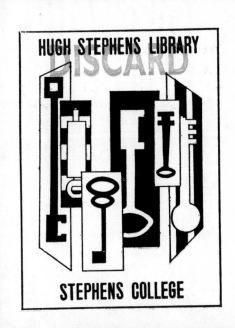

Books by Marya Zaturenska

POETRY

The Hidden Waterfall
Collected Poems
Terraces of Light
Selected Poems
The Golden Mirror
The Listening Landscape
Cold Morning Sky
Threshold and Hearth

PROSE

A Gallery of Poets (In Progress)
Christina Rossetti: A Portrait with Background
A History of American Poetry, 1900–1940
(With Horace Gregory)

ANTHOLOGIES

Selected Poems of Christina Rossetti: with introduction
Collected Poems of Sara Teasdale: with introduction
The Crystal Cabinet: An Introduction to Poetry
(With Horace Gregory)
The Silver Swan: Poems of Mystery and Imagination
(With Horace Gregory)
The Mentor Book of Religious Verse
(With Horace Gregory)
Love's Cross-Currents by A. C. Swinburne,
with a critical essay by Marya Zaturenska

MARYA
ZATURENSKA

The Hidden Waterfall

POEMS

The Vanguard Press, Inc.
New York

"Chorale for the Seasons," "Homage to Christina Rossetti," "Spellbound," "The World of the Salamanders,"
and "Metaphysics of the Night," from Collected
Poems by Marya Zaturenska. Copyright © 1970 by
Marya Zaturenska Gregory. Reprinted by kind permission of the Viking Press, Inc.
    "Perdita's Song" and "Miranda's Song" first ap-
peared in the New York Times. Copyright © 1970 by
Marya Zaturenska Gregory. Reprinted by permission
of the New York Times.
    "Sentimental Colloquy," "The Vision of Dido,"
"Prospero's Soliloquy," "The Bird and the Muse"
were first published in the September, 1973 issue of
Poetry. Copyright © 1973 by Marya Zaturenska.

Epigraph "We shall not cease from exploration . . ."
from "Little Gidding" in FOUR QUARTETS by
T. S. Eliot. Copyright 1942, 1943 by T. S. Eliot; renewed 1970 by Esme Valerie Eliot. Reprinted by permission of Harcourt Brace Jovanovich, Inc.

Designer: Ernst Reichl
Manufactured in the United States of America

For Judith and Robert Phillips

and as always
for
Horace Gregory

We shall not cease from exploration
And the end of all our exploring
Will be to arrive where we started
And know the place for the first time.
Through the unknown, remembered gate . . .
The voice of the hidden waterfall

—T. S. Eliot,
Four Quartets

CONTENTS

A Shakespearean Cycle

The Traveler

An Italian Garland

Illuminations & Pastorals

A Shakespearean Cycle

I
Prospero's Soliloquy

Loud sounds the clock. I sit at home,
Free from tempests and mad storms.
Years have consumed me, passions worn.
My island sinks in sea and sand;
It drifts away—is No Man's Land.

Mystery shields me like a cloak,
Envelops me in my last age,
Robs me of my rich heritage—
The ever-living earth and air—
Strips me of longing and of care—
Drained of patience—hard as bone—
I now am free, am now alone.

In savage silence, spirit-guided,
When voices rose from harassed caves
I mastered men with alchemy;
I fettered wild beasts: through my law
They knelt, they feared, became my slaves.

Released from longing, sadness, shame,
From hatred festering in my breast,
I, who have known the worst and best,
Can gaze unmoved on all I see:
The fruitless triumph, or disgrace,
Injustice, and its haunted face.

The shipwreck on the madman's coast,
The ravaged wail, the spirit's sigh,
The sorrow of the long oppressed,
I shall remember till I die;
To have escaped much is my boast.

All evil done, in part undone—
My forfeit kingdom, lost and won,
I love at last, and can condone
All bitterness for a child's sake.
The quiet light that the stars make
Can bless at last, can now atone.

Voice sounding through the wounded air,
Set free of pride and vanity,
The stars at night will shelter me.
I break my wand, disown my powers,
Sunlight and awe, and creeping hours—
Shed is the anger, striving, pain.
I sail to exile once again.

II
Perdita's Song

Cast, cast, adrift, disowned, disowning
You seek your father and your mother,
Too far from the safe tomb
You drift too long and drift forever
Under the willow-weeping grove,
Under the golden-gleaming orange tree,
Where shall you find your home?

The storm, in silent anguish rising,
Will strike your island's sleeping heart.
The rescuers seek but have not found you.
Soon the mastering tides will creep—
No voice shall bless, no eyes behold
Your glassy fountain's frozen wonder
Beneath whose silenced charm you lie.

Red is the moon, the cloud's unfolding
The lovely view no eye beholds;
Unshared the golden lamps of morning,
Unseen the silver bowl of night
Where the stars fall unloved, uncaring,
Where no heart bleeds, where no tears fall:
There let the great storm break.

III
Cordelia's Song

Only the unloved know
The wild reach of the heart,
Vulnerable, sick with rage
That no word can assuage
So desperate is fate,
So inarticulate.

Did I not plead again
To the lost man in the rain,
Appealed to him in vain,
Forever tried to prove
That love was truly love,
Though wrung so clumsily
From the heart of pain.

Dearer than salt, than bread,
Your arrow in my breast
When life seemed weariest;
That love so strong, so deep,
So difficult, unkind,
Fell like a star or flower
In caverns of the mind,
Blind, dark, and steep.

IV
Mariana's Song

Wind on the aging house
Set in an emerald sea
Of summer-waving grass. . . .
When will my deliverer pass,
For whom I wait and wait
In mingled love and hate?
What will become of me?

There was a promise in the hall,
A messenger at the gate—
Some tokens came too late.
Soon, soon the forgotten stair
Sounds to a lost footfall.
Will he come to call?

Lonely is the house,
Within the moated grange
Nothing will ever change.
Time echoes everywhere.
The clock chimes with an eerie
Languishing despair—
No one is ever there.
I sit and comb my hair.

The book falls from my hand
(An old tale is retold),
The flower dies in the glass,
It was thirsty and grew old:
It was undone
Without air, or sun.

Was that a knock on the door
Or a leaf falling?
Was it his voice I heard
Faltering, calling?
Morning is gone: the dark
Silence appalling.

Swimming in golden air,
In whispering, willow-waving summer grass,
Year after year the world springs up,
Fills with a clear green wine
My life's untasted cup,
Fantasies fester and thrive.
He will never arrive.

In that locked tower
Dust fell on my bright hair.
Sharp through the long corridors
I hear the creaking of unopened doors.
Was it the wind, or my fate
That made me wait,
Or bestial footsteps on the crumbling stair?

Iron-corroded sun
Seen through cracked window glass—
How fluid and free the shimmering twilight's gleam
In some unworldly dream of hill and stream
Where the wild deer unhurt, unhunted, run.

V

Ophelia's Song

Eyes of despair, eyes of fire,
Watchful terror, warlike peace.
Quenched is the star of all desire:
It sings the song of my release.
I throw fresh garlands, white and red,
Into the devouring river bed.

The willows shiver as I pass.
I feel the trembling of the grass.
As the waves rise, and slide, and fall,
I sink through islands of dark water.

None shall remember, few recall
The early Spring's unhappy daughter
Whom amorous Death found loveliest.

No Prince can claim me, and no charm
Scoop from the waters my small flowers.
They drown in running wave and stream—
Pale Undines of some idle hours—
Lost in the willows' drowning gleam.

My floating, underwater bed,
My little garland, white and red,
Will know my name. The willows shed
Familiar shadows on my head.

As the flowers and the stream
Sink deep in elemental calm—
And the song, and the dream . . .

I shall not come to harm.

VI
Miranda's Song

To my island, late returning,
Since my life's meridian source
Shrinks in silence, silent music
Draws me hither.

Forms of beauty long departed,
Snake-green rivers lithely weaving,
All my flower-fine youth reviving,
And the dwindling moon
Kills the memory of rich cities,
Worldly manners, charming strangers;
On this island let my morning
Soul its early music render.

How clear the springs! the forsaken island—
There the earliest winds caress me,
It is late, the jasmine blossoms
Fall like snow on fading tresses.

The Traveler

The Traveler

As the locked room devours me and the sun
Falls russet and gold upon the autumnal streets,
The mind releases its flights, runs, flies, retreats.

The mind is a great traveler, sleeping it awakes
Enormous worlds, scenes open to the blind,
Plants dropped into the earth, or seeded in the mind.

Islands of oblivion sunk in deserted caves,
Lost gold of Mycenae, earthbound labyrinths of Crete,
Atlantis underseas, that myth or legend saves.

They appear through the buried night, dim struggling light
The tall towers of Atlantis, green as jade
To siren song they rise, then fade from sight.

Clarity, peace, and delight, that lives on desire and strives
Where once loomed cataracts, nightmares, trackless spaces,
As through a mist we see our contracted lives
Reflected in a thousand dreamless faces.

We learn at last how desperate, faltering, fainting,
The early heavens grew deep with purest blue,
A flush of peach trees, blooming, sudden, graces,
Delights our eyes, the beautiful is true.

We see the world as in a Chinese painting;
From world to world we glide from plain to plain.

The willow trees are bending in the rain.

A Spring of Tears

(after a refrain from Christine de Pisan, 1365–1431?)

A spring of tears, a river brimming over,
Sadness moving through milk-pale skies,
Stronger than the river Seine, the young wind is blowing
A spring of tears, a river brimming over.

Plunged into longing for what has not been
The rain is weeping. O the April rain
Falling softly, falling on man, beast, flower,
A dreaming and a life-bestowing shower,
A spring of tears, a river brimming over.

For the mountains of glass that the skies uncover,
For the estates of heaven where the white angels gleam—
For the drowned worlds I have never known,
For pastures never tended or sown,
A spring of tears, a river brimming over.

For the tall towers of the city seen in sleep
A longing, a longing, hostile and deep,
To climb its monuments so high and steep,
To hesitate, to wonder, and to leap—
A spring of tears, a river brimming over.

Once in an Ancient Book

Once, in an ancient book,
Remembering what I read,
Lines scattered to the wind
Or buried in the sand,
Words quoted, widely spread,
Now lost to humankind
In a dry, dead land,

Still, still, some glory thrives,
Blooms and has many lives,
Through deepest memory
Retains strange influence—glows
In clear serenity
Through longing or repose.

It tells how beauty flows
In some obscure delight
Through pain, through failing sight,
Through subterranean streams
Of love, through the very soul
Longing to be made whole,
Or sees the dark made bright—
Sees also from a height
Some secret goal.

The World of the Salamanders

Slowly, and one by one, with few to see or hear
Above the chilling movement of the sea
The salamanders dripping gold appear.

Through trembling waters, over primal seas
They arise, and sing of fire, of fire-lit fantasies;
They summon marvels, legends, mysteries.

Then arise at their command from wind and wave
Divas, Peris, water-pale Undines
And mist-veiled weeping queens.

In wavering worlds of sleep, in the skull's cave they sing
A *gloria* in honor of their king.

The Witching Hour

Shadows of trees in the rocky millstream gleam
A pallid silver where the dying moon
Scatters the moonlight mist and bows their branches,
Twisted and thin they lean.

Dark, intertwined, they tumble in the stream;
They drown and dip, they fall and drown again,
They shed their freshness on the frail wildflowers,
The thirsty woodland, and the neighboring grass—
This is the witching hour.

Night like a runner speeds in wind and water.
The dawn will rise, young light made manifest.
Too soon, hot daylight will consume my rest;
I know the longing for the unpossessed.
And where the murmuring winds and waters sigh,
Pale as the moon I lie
In fruitless fantasy.

Lost is the image that appeared to me,
Lost in the expanding light's lucidity,
But now through mist-dark landscape, vapor, cloud,
The flying nightingale sings aloud.

Another Snowstorm

Do you remember, dear friend, the many snowstorms
We have endured? in a worn, too fragile house
How long could it last? We were trapped in cold,
We had seen so little of the sun,
So few of the glittering stars,
We never missed what we had always known
And now, another snow.

But the granary is full and the harvest sown.

Always through shaded windows beauty shone,
Despair played a music strange and clear,
We wrote it down;
Hope built a cheerful pathway for our feet.
We never knew defeat.

Now we are free of fear
In the white whirlwind of the year.
What we have feared came shamefaced and lame,
So worn, so tame,
We had forgotten its name.

But we knew that the Spring flowers would come again
Soon, ah, soon,
The small white flowers unhaunted by the moon,
Or the winter night,
Being so fragrant and bright.

Soon, soon the melting snow
And the air fresh and still,
Again the hyacinth and daffodil,
The little snowdrop growing in the rain—
We too begin again
Beyond pleasure or pain.

Chorale for the Seasons

In the time of the scorpion we first came
To the forests floating in light, and the swaying shadows
Sun-dipped in moving gold,
Leaving despair behind, and a dark season,
The sting of malice, and the dangerous door,
O my bright scorpion!

Beautiful it was in the year of the Ram,
The wildflowers opening in love to the sun, the trees wavered
Warm in trembling air, fanning the sea-blue heaven:
There the children were always in white, and always singing,
O my beautiful ones!
Time drew her curtain down, and veiled the scene.

It was best to live in the time of the running deer,
Soft-eyed and wary, peering behind dark thickets
Or leaping through mist-wrapped mountains, drinking in cool
    hollows,
O my doe with the fearful eyes!
It was your year of illusion, white is your shade on the mountain.

Slowly we wheeled into the cycle of the wild swans
When the rain flooded the earth, and the children departing
Spread their soft wings to the light, ascended to thundering
    heavens;
Left alone to the quiet of the moon, to the whirling waters,
Beautiful swans, we salute you—
Flying into the unknown, landing in virgin skyscapes,
Exploring unborn stars.

Drifting, sauntering, see we have reached
The world of the water lilies.
Only in dreams, when the spirit, released, leaves her unwanted
    body,
When the sun is obscured, and the night prepares
To unveil her starry shores—
In the white trance of the moon,
O my white and golden lilies!

Now is the time when the demon that hides in the clouds,
The seawraiths that wail in the waters,
The storm spirits chained in the shaking woods
Mix with the scorpions, mate with the wild swans,
Call to the golden Ram who grows fat in a prosperous meadow;
Timid, the white doe drinks, returns to the shimmering pool
Where the young stars are drowning.
Drift like the stars, my soul,
My white and drifting lily.

Love Song

Gone the great torment for the sacred grove
Where lovers bathe in blithe, immortal streams
And watch the brief, the vanishing star that gleams
In one bright flash of neural ecstasy.

Still, through my dwindling years, I seem to see
The one beloved walking in bright air,
And where he walks fresh springs and waterfalls,
The dew-bright foliage of an early Spring,
Surround, enclose the world's felicity.

What, who is this that freshens the new grass?
Whose is the voice summoning waterfalls?
The enchanted deer that haunts the forbidden forest?
Splendor and joy where the young fawns run
On an untrodden lawn?

And who is this that calls up the new dawn,
And makes the flowers bloom near the waterfall,
Fragile and gay when the dark day is done,
And the expanding heart drinks in the sun?

A Young Girl Singing

Through summer-sparkling days, when skies were bright,
In a white dress through a green stream of light
I walked in a naked world as if by candlelight
And heard through the wind-twisted blaze of the trees
That a new voice was crying in the sea-cold breeze;
As the grass, flowing like green water to my knees,
Ran in a rising stream of joy and praise
Of the sun-flooded, champagne-dizzy days,
Of the grass blowing and rising into a green-gold maze.
And the young voice that spoke through an invisible horn
Was the dry forest voice of the not-yet-born,
A voice like a fresh leaf from a green tree torn!

Water Lilies: A Nocturne

Once water lilies floated on this pool.
Now they are gone, only their phantoms sigh,
Only an old song to recall them by,
Only the memory of a world that flew
So fast and long ago that memories cool.

Gone are the lilies that I gazed upon
With the fond eyes of youth, the lilies white and fine,
To sadder, darker days I now resign
The weeping reeds that stand line upon line,
Grim relics of a world once fresh and new.

The midnight visions and the morning gleams
So rich with sunlight, starlight and bright streams.

Only the wild fowls of the marshes call,
Only the thin brown reeds hold festival,
And I return, a shadow tamed and small,
Frail as the reeds, as mortal and as pale
Beneath the moon, beneath the moonlight's trail.

From
"The Madness of Jean Jacques Rousseau"
(*a poem in progress*)

Who reads my book reads all my life,
Who reads my countenance sees all my soul,
Come all who see, who feel, who read, who love,
Know that the heart is pure though the flesh fail,
Though the blood runs darkly to an impure sea.

I stand where Alpine torrents find their source,
Near lakes of fire that burn eternally,
Conspiring malice in its secret force
Destroys, torments me, casts me in that sea.

But born near Alpine mountains I can live
Lifted above my sins, I still can stand
A hated prophet in a hostile land
Through hatred and destruction far above
Alert and naked, eager to win love.

Why do averted eyes still follow me?
Deep at the center gleams the fatal flaw.

Theme from a Poem by Boris Pasternak

Remember, Lord, the wedding feast
And the guests who welcomed You,
Recall the bridegroom and the bride
Who knelt in homage at Your side
Before Your dream was crucified.

Betrayal, anguish, sorrow, doubt
Will come, will pierce Your open heart—
But this one moment lives apart—
This is Your moment. All adore.

Adoring You, the old, the sick,
The lonely drained of warmth and love,
The innocent, the dull, the wise
Live in Your life-enhancing eyes;
The dead will listen, and the quick,

The homeless, hopeless, bring their sighs,
Envy's slow poison, traitor's kiss,
Will reach Your final loneliness—
But take this moment's transient bliss.

The bridegroom and the bride kneel down.
In permanence Your blessing spreads
And spreads to each unblesséd town
The healing fire that is Your own.

Alas, the poor, the old, the sick,
The lost who never left Your side,
They never left You, they abide—
Who sought Your blessing on their knees
Who drank the last wine to the lees,

Who when the others left still stayed
And followed You when others fled—
They cherished You. But what of those
Who heard the truth You died to tell,
Who sneered at every miracle—
Whom You could heal, yet could not save
Though Lazarus rose from his grave!

The Wound and the Arrow

(a fragment)

It was in a savage cradle you were laid
Where you were rocked to sleep by night and day
To the star's wonder and the sun's dismay,
Where the city like a tropic forest lay
And you unlocked your hopes, bartered your soul.
Force leads you through the evolving stars that roll
World upon worlds. The amber sun has sprayed
Its violent heat upon you and your view,
A barren landscape bright with morning dew.

A savage woman climbed the star-bound mountain,
In her hand she carried the bow that will pierce your mind
And open the wound that will wean you from mankind.

The Young Dancers

Now the reviving sea
Returns in summer waves
Where the young dancers fled
Whose image time engraves
(From some lost long ago)
Because of some gift, some grace,
That death could not deface.

Slow their approach, so slow,
We watch with anxious heart.
Nightfall they knew, and snow,
Have they forgotten their part?
It was their fate to play
A lifelong holiday.

Nightfall came soon, and snow
Descended on each head,
The known world turned to stone,
All the spectators gone,
In a forgotten place
Each played their role alone.

Restored to youth again
By the time-tide's force,
Life, like an untamed horse,
Runs the exciting shore.
Fine mind and exquisite face
Resume their cherished place,
They find their old allies.
Rare beauty never dies—
The dancers come once more.

In the keen air, in the sun's fire,
In an implacable desire
Renewed are the sea's advances
Resume, resume, the old dances,
And the song with the old refrain,
Renew our life again!

An Italian Garland

For Bryher

I
Hymn to Poseidon

White palaces arise
On that historic sea
That floats to Orient lands.
Fabled, their luster gone,
Still they invoke the one
Sea Goddess who arises
First on a sunnier sea.

She laves her green-gold hair
Unveils her rose-pale limbs
On the thin sea shell
And floats to stronger waves. . . .

Then calls to Poseidon,
The father of the deep,
To rouse his realm from sleep,
Bids wind and water keep
That sky-blue trance forever
While the embracing sea
Surrounds the crumbling strand
And Loves and Saints and Nymphs
And Angels mount each tower
In renewed power.

Then startled forms arise
Wind-twisted, coral-damp,
Warm amber stained with brine,
Forms monstrous and marine,
But you, St. Mark, have held
Your city in your hand,
The winged lion at your side.

43

II
After the Italian of Claudio Achillini
(1614–1640)

Wars and of arms some sing, but I
Of other battles, wounds, and victories sing
The sound of men embattled and their cry;
No, not to these has my warm spirit turned,
I sing of Love, a warrior tall and fair
Who brought me all the sorrow that I knew
And all the beautiful, the good, the true;
Tell then, my heart, how you were vanquishéd,
Transfixed, and troubled by a lock of hair
And tell how many angry tears I shed
For a harsh look from two cold mocking eyes
(More fatal in their killing glance than Mars'
Whose victories are as potent and as strong.)

'Tis *Amor*, *Amor* who has vanquished me,
He whom the seas extol, life's living rhythm praise,
He kills my heart but gives life to my song,
He shortens, but gives meaning to my days.

III
After the Italian of Lorenzo de' Medici
(1448 – 1492)

Leave, Cytherea, your enchanted isle,
Remote, green-shaded is that Paradise:
Its crisp-cool waters, its rain-jeweled showers,
Its fountains rising to the ravished eyes. . . .
Rest, white-limbed Goddess, while the magic waters
Multiply into fountains, sky-drawn springs,
Bathe in the rose-faint heavens while the clouds sail,
Move with the sun and hear the Sirens sing,
The fountains answer, and the streams prolong
That song of air, of water-wavering clouds.

Swan-guarded, close-locked world, O Cytherea,
Eternity at peace is mortal here,
Lured by the silver breath of purest song—
See how the love-lost seek your land and long
To claim the vistas of delight, they bring
The Sun-Seeker, he who leads them all,
Your laughing son, young Eros, winged and tall.

IV
After the Italian of Torquato Tasso
(1544–1595)

White moon, star-strewn sky,
Night's mantle now is thrown
On you and the turning earth;
The darkening universe,
Seen through a crystal ring,
Gleams with a cloudy pallor.

Stars drop on the dark grass,
The empty silence dreams,
The wind withholds its voice
But trembles in the air.
The locked heart hears the sound:
Midnight now appears,
How cold the night, how cold!

Something is waiting here,
I hear it in the dark,
In the pale light of the moon
My sorrow will not pass.
A knife, moon-silver sharp,
Is thrust into my heart,
I feel but cannot bleed—

O life of my life!

46

V

Portrait of Her Lover
After the Italian of Gaspara Stampa
(1523–1554)

Ladies who ask me to portray my love,
The Lord who rules my world of whom I sing,
Picture him young, gay, elegant, erect,
Gay, witty, learned, high-bred, O everything
Youthful in years, mature in intellect,
Well-versed in men and books, skilled in the wars.

By what conjunction have our conflicting stars
Brought us together under Amor's wing
(Delightful God whose faith ebbs like the sea)
With him whose graces Jove rains from above,
Knowing perfection how it flies from me?

And ladies whom my portrait too must see
If honesty must guide a faltering tongue,
Tell of a face by passion marred and crossed,
By Death's strong image, haggard, tempest-tossed,
No longer worshiped and no longer young,
(The charming manner, the beguiling tongue)
Torn between longing for my love and grave.

A woman sick of silence and dry days
Whom neither tears, fame, eloquence can save,
Who dies forever in love's chilling gaze.

VI
After the Italian of Vincenzo Monti
(1754 – 1823)

A coward thought has struck me: "See poor soul
How learning and the inner vision fail
And the red earth spins on, and night
Begins to drown, to dim the hopeful day—
The beloved faces smile but will not stay."

Then I replied: "And if my outer sight
Is lost, what harm is there? I see
A clearer, cleaner, a more dazzling light
That still embraces earth, explores the sky,
All things assume the heavenly shape; I see
The flying Beauty that has ravished me,
Fame and oblivion to Her are one,
Seen through Her eyes the pursuit of fame
Appears a childish thing. I woo the Sun."

Illuminations & Pastorals

Sentimental Colloquy
(*after Verlaine*)

In pine forests, rain-misted, shadowed, cold,
They pass who lived and died with time grown old.
Dead are their eyes and cold, their garments damp with dew,
Estranged from earth and sky, they come to a strange rendezvous.

Solitary spreads the green, wide-stretching park,
Eyes meet and hearts awake, again they come;
Facing each other their cold hearts are numb.

Do you remember how we loved this place
When all my life reached forth to greet your face?
Do you remember it?
No. I forget.

But here a sleeping world burst into flame.
All, all desire lived in your living name,
Each blade of grass drank light, each tree aglow,
Do you remember? *No.*

The heartbeats dying away so long ago—
Even that autumn where gold leaves lay rotten
I have forgotten.

The hopes, the years, the joys unspeakable
When lyric springs, cool rains, were not impossible?
Wind-fresh, aerial-cool, the icebound waters flow
Into youth's springtime? Do you remember? *No.*

Vanished are the laurels standing fresh and high,
Forgotten is the grief and overcast the sky.
The land we knew is gone, and memory dimmed and tame,
Falling are the leaves, our throats are choked and dry.
Cannot you spare a sigh?
Not I.

These two return, seeking their ancient walk,
Only the night receives them, only two strangers talk.

Hidden Thunder: A Corot Landscape

Were there rose-skirted nymphs lifting their arms
To reach the topmost branches of the trees?
There were no golden apples shining there,
No falling star, no azure-breasted bird.
Once they were there, but fled in a light breeze,
And once a star fell when soft shadows stirred.

Heroes in armor cast an occult spell:
Swan-knights and dancing dogs left long ago,
But hidden thunder and a rumor of snow
Spoke in a threatening voice we never heard
Of a silver-circled charm
Of grace and motion stirring mind and eyes
And somewhere a faint hint of Paradise.

Spirits of earth and air, of mist and cloud,
Threatened at first and then sang out aloud
Of worlds unborn, of rare felicity,
A clouded past, a harsh futurity,
Myth, fear, or prophecy.

Time, like an early April, lingered there,
Colored the air and mind. Vibration shook the trees,
The thunder came too close, but never fell,
Caught in a sudden spell—
Nothing dazzled the eyes or lifted the hair.
The stars in furtive shine
Marched in bright procession, line on line,
And the rose-nymphs' lifted arms
Evoked an encircling charm.

This water-misted landscape stayed too long,
Beauty and magic glazed in memory,
The shifting worlds sunk deep in undersea
Clung to a child's heart
But in its after ages played a part.
Always the nymphs will dance beneath that tree,
Daughters of air and the young April green,
Virgin attendants of the moon queen.
They dance like the stars, like the young leaves,
The coming storm descends, it sings and grieves.

The Vision of Dido

There Dido stood again—
In her drenched garments, pale against the torches
Held by the attendant ghosts who followed her
Flickering in timid shadow, mothlike forms
(Through the dim cavelights of eternal Hades)
Half drowsy, half alive, but half immortal—
There the dead live till the true word is spoken
And there Aeneas stood.

In a low voice chilled by the underworld
She spoke again as if remembrance failed,
And the armed warrior thought of funeral pyres,
His faithless love, her anguish, his betrayal—
Pleaded with her, as if the indifferent Gods
Were speaking through him.

"Forgive, since in my sin the Gods contrived,
The Gods whom Destiny obeys, who mold our deeds
Beyond our will, beyond the might-have-been,
For only they create our lives to be
Firm to create, or kill."

The torches flickered, the attendant shadows dimmed,
She stood alone in a mild flame of light
Cast from the sailing moon, her face was stone,
An archaic image in a sinking world.
Passionless, heedless, thoughtless as the moon
Memory rose again, then flowed away
In the blind gaze that neither feels nor sees.

Her silence surged from buried memory;
Neither forgiveness ruled, nor outraged passion,
Neither the vision of her funeral pyre,
Her happy leap into embracing fire
Ascending to wild skies on Carthage hill.

Then, in that calm that is not pain or peace,
The sullen Lethe rose in darkening tide;
She slowly stared at him, then turned and fled
And left him lonely, lost, unrecognized.

Lament of Katherine Howard,
Fifth Queen of Henry VIII

Happy in the sparkling green,
In the Maytime of my years,
Suddenly I saw the sky
Like crisp water, running clear,
Brightly, freshly, running clear.

For a feather in my cap,
For a ribbon in my hair,
For a jewel at my throat,
I had dared life's highest stair—
Life so young and debonair.

Then I met my aging king,
Rich and heavy, lustful, strong,
Easy ran my lute, each string
Wind and water, wave, prolong
Rich and rolling in the hall,
In the mirrored gallery
Rang the golden-timbred song.

To the violin and the lute
I have danced the sun away,
Danced away my life and soul,
Danced old England fast away,
Danced away my new-found years,
Blood and violence and tears.

In the old king's tainted bed,
Still my blood danced, youth and joy
Held a moment like a toy
Till the tainted blood grew cool
In the crimson damasked bed,
All my wanton moments fled.

Lust has dried the sparkling well
Of my dancing summertime;
Power, intrigue, dissolved the spell
'Twixt the bridegroom and the bride.
Weep for silly, pretty things,
Pleasure doomed to foul mishap
For a frock, a jewel, a ring,
For a flower on my cap.

Yet my true love doomed with me.
An iron house of constancy
Shields us both eternally,
Shields us from the fatal king,
Though this fate I have deserved
I have kept our parting vow,
"None shall ever say I swerved:
Time and the grave destroy and sever—
Constancy remains forever."

The Invaders

A child runs in to play,
The child grown, now away,
The child that haunts my heart
By night, by day

Whose image fills the room,
Enveloping my days,
Engrossing all my ways,
Source of all prayers I raise.

The children grow, my flesh
Withdraws from the bright room,
The days, the days, unwind
My hopes, my fears, I find

Dream children dance and sway,
Enter my room and play
And when I leave they stay
By night or day.

Soon will the young fawn drink
Deep in the silver stream,
Soon will the morning sink
In a cold, pristine dream,

Soon will the children fly
Worlds upon worlds away—
But still they haunt my heart
By night, by day.

A Winter Journal

Blow your trumpets too! Memory,
Mother of all the Muses, answers you
Who now her classic wreath and tunic drops
And naked as the morning sky she stands,
The golden trumpet in her snow-veined hands.
Withdrawn Goddess, Nymph of the submerged fountain,
Mother of History, Queen of the fluid stream
Wherein the story of our race abides,
From your long secret eyes our vision speaks
And the fluid truth more intricate is seen—
An eternal comment on life's changing scene—
The violet-frail, the delicate mystery
Of the great tides, the ever restless sea,
Rocks worn by ceaseless pressure, the buried city
Sunk under lava, burning all life away
Or swept through the long reaches of the sea
In a cold fury without pity
Whether the marine world veils its plunder or
The white rose in the garden sways as it glows
Through the veiled Eyes where all compassion flows.

Here Where the Gold Is Dark

For Tobias Bolton Gregory

Here where the gold is dark who shall awake
The gold and silver rivers in our dream?
Sleep on, it is the sunny season, sleep;
Sleep, child, with the red-gold hair, whose sea-green eyes
Blend with sea darkness when the morning breaks.

Dawn summons silver swans, brings up the floods
Of singing summer in its gay excess;
The darkness blends with solar light, green hoods
Are drawn across the vernal lids of joy
And for a while Time's fertile, rich excess
Rises to spray with light, to rejoice, to bless.

My dear with the red-gold hair, sun-dazzling boy,
Time flowers toward you, and gleaming as I turn
The blanched blue foxgloves, the red carnations burn.

O Like a Young Tree

O like a young tree rooted near the water,
Foreseeing the fresh season, year by year
So let me stand.

Like the suave moss, grown thick on water's edge,
Warm under the tree's root, cooled by the driving wave
Let me endure.

Surprising, dewy bright as the wild strawberry
In leaves that form a basket green and fine
As ruddy and gay.

Or the June rose that springs up new and sweet,
Bride of the summer, child of summer rains
So fair adorned.

The lake-clear heart, fern-fresh, the brimming look
To face the dark, and the clear happy eyes
Of lake-drowned stars.

Let me ensnare for a leaf's span, for a flower's season
Joy's rosy, transient wing skied in the summer light
Warm and unshadowed.

I Know an Island

I know an island, pale in the green sea
Where the Atlantic waves grow lost in mist,
Of delicate violet and pure amethyst,
Where the gray sea gulls rise monotonously.

Green, green the shoreline, rises cool and green,
The trees green, black, against a somber sky
Small purpling hills archaic and serene
Through lingering rains that fall deep, endlessly.

Step on this greenest, softest, dreamiest turf
To breathe the mystery this isle presents
And you shall hear the sound of violence
Subdued and hostile as the rising surf.

Saints, heroes, kings, and martyrs, waxed and waned
In this their ancient seat, gray-toned yet wild
In haggard beauty, subtle as a child,
How many times adored, subdued, profaned.

Possession

What bed is that from which the dead arise?
Their voices speak to the dry, the withering hearts
Who wander away from the world, cheerfully and apart,
The beautiful sent to the dark too early cannot depart
Without some pact with life, and as the cold waves rang
On the fine-tuned soul that expired as the stars sang,
Felt through dark and cold, the song of the slipping sun
In a thread-thin, hair-gold, vermilion.

With your quick active limbs you now arise,
And shaking off the inactive centuries
Feel through the earth trapped quiet the old wound
Or see the cloudy moon swim underground,
Learn how the lusts, scents, music can return
To that great bed where all lost ardors burn
Fine eyes, warm limbs, perturb the sleeping mind
That slept so long, so deep, so unresigned.

Spellbound

I looked and saw your life
In the shadow of your hair,
In the glory of your eyes—
Bells, bells rang everywhere
On the storm-threatened air.

I looked and saw a light
In the shadow of your brow,
In the white power of your hand,
A whirl of wind and snow
Where golden angels stand
Gleaming against the night.

This was the moment when trees
Lifted their April arms
In a pale rush of green
Shading a moonlit scene
Casting their early charms
And their new-born dreams
In magic streams.

O then it was I saw
In the shadow of your hair,
In the dark power of your eyes,
The magnetic pull of the sea—
Earth's spellbound mystery
Strict in its changing law.

Metaphysics of the Night

Our bones are scattered at the grave's mouth,
Our lives have fled before the certain tread
Of Time, she of the multiple disguises, she
Who in her many forms is never still.

How fresh and gay among the daffodils
In the April season by a gleaming river
We saw her first, quick, ardent, saffron-robed,
Free as the air, a dryad with sunstruck hair
Who moved in a green world, plucking white flowers.

White rose on fire! moss rose in a damp meadow
She seemed—firebright in a burning season,
Green world on fire! air's freedom lightly shadowed,
Immortality in modern dress appears
Disguised as Time, was Time, is Time itself,
A gay green masquer in a crumbling world.

And now invisible among the stars
I hear her in the murmers of the tide
Gliding through rain-soaked branches in the park
Hovering over banquets and the dance.

And violet-shadowed in the receding sea
And darkening mild Sunday afternoons
Her sable image rises and restores
Solitude, certitude, and history.

Homage to Christina Rossetti

Silence of after-wars, when through the air
The high, leaf-dropping tree
Reflects the bright blue weather glowing there,
So still, so quiet your fame, diffused, yet nowhere:

Your dark Italian streams of English song
Poured such clear fountains down,
Delicate as a string of fine-matched pearls, as strong
As the fretted iron in the great Tuscan's crown;

And fresh as young-eyed seasons of the mind
When the heart bathes in sun and clouded streams grow clearer,
Or when the grave and golden autumns find
God's contemplative beauty closer, nearer.

Then best we praise you for your garlands' shading,
Death's feet and Love's, garlands of small, perfect roses,
Small roses few but perfect, never fading,
Brought from your secret heavens, startling our garden closes.

For you the Sacred Muse revealed her illumined way
And taught the single heart, devout and true,
How to praise God in fire-touched songs that pray,
Songs that Teresa heard, Siena's Catherine knew.

Then, like a garland of pearls or a night sky, huge and cold,
Or a great pillar of fire, or a small, wounded bird,
Your quiet gifts rang purest gold,
Rang finest silver, and were loved, were heard.

Bird and the Muse

The Muse that stirs my blood,
In unforeseen control
Takes form, becomes a bird
Blazing through realms of gold,

Leaves me so suddenly
I hardly know her gone,
In worlds remote from me
She flies through land and sea.

Although the unwilling soul
Shrinks from her brilliant flight
She must fulfill her role
Resume her mythic part
Enter the sleeping heart.

Write then although the walls
Close in with never a sound,
She chides, inspires, recalls
The rarely trodden ground.

Learn patiently to paint
The white face of your God
In the indifferent night
When all the senses faint.

She may again appear
Through heart and soul and mind
When your two eyes are blind
And days are dulled in fear.

Poor, lonely, her reward
The angelic note of praise
Your life must not record
Through all your days.

The Flying Victory
Lifts wounded wings, and sings,
Part Goddess and part bird,
I hear her passing sigh,
Her final whisperings.